COFFEE ART

Creative coffee designs
for the home barista

Dhan Tamang
★★ Five times UK Latte Art Champion ★★

CASSELL
ILLUSTRATED

An Hachette UK Company
www.hachette.co.uk

First published in Great Britain in 2017
by Cassell, a division of Octopus Publishing
Group Ltd, Carmelite House, 50 Victoria
Embankment, London EC4Y 0DZ
www.octopusbooks.co.uk
www.octopusbooksusa.com

Text copyright © Dhan Tamang 2017
Design and layout copyright © Octopus
Publishing Group Ltd 2017

Distributed in the US by Hachette Book Group,
1290 Avenue of the Americas, 4th and 5th
Floors, New York, NY 10104

Distributed in Canada by Canadian Manda
Group, 664 Annette St., Toronto, Ontario,
Canada M6S 2C8

Dhan Tamang asserts the moral right to be
identified as the author of this work.

ISBN 978-1-84403-948-7

A CIP catalogue record for this book
is available from the British Library.

Printed and bound in China.

1 3 5 7 9 10 8 6 4 2

Publishing Director: Trevor Davies
Art Director: Yasia Williams-Leedham
Senior Editor: Leanne Bryan
Copy Editor: Abi Waters
Photographer: Jason Ingram
Designer: Sally Bond
Production Controller: Sarah Kulasek-Boyd

Additional text by Leanne Bryan,
Ellie Corbett, Trevor Davies
and Abi Waters.

Contents

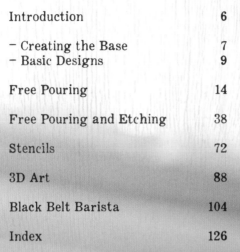

Introduction

Originally from Kathmandu in Nepal, I have been in the UK for six years, after moving here to learn all I could about coffee. Since my first job as a barista, I have loved the world of coffee. What better job is there than being able to make my customers smile every day by presenting them with their coffee and an extra special design?

The longer I work with coffee, the stronger my passion grows. I'm always eager to learn more about this craft and want to travel the world to learn more and share my knowledge. My diligence and passion has lead to me win the UK Latte Art Champion award five times and I'd now like to share my passion and ideas with you at home with the fantastic designs in this book.

The most fantastic coffee art really is possible for any home barista with just a little patience and practice. The designs in this book will show you how to create picture-perfect artworks on top of your coffee. From elegant designs to fabulous 3D sculptures, you will be able to learn everything from mastering the basic coffee pouring skills through to more complex black belt barista designs. There are more than 60 designs to try and by the end of this book you will be able to free pour, etch, stencil and sculpt stunning images, which will delight dinner party guests and family members alike.

What equipment do I need?

There is very little equipment you need to be able to create coffee art, but here is a rundown of the basics:

★ A coffee machine to make espresso.
★ A milk frother – these can be as basic or as expensive as you can afford and will be used to steam and froth milk to make your lattes, cappuccinos and babyccinos. You may have a full coffee machine with a steaming wand to meet all your needs, but you can achieve the same results using a basic milk frother.
★ A pouring jug – to pour the steamed and frothed milk into your espresso.
★ A selection of coffee cups in different sizes – ranging from small espresso cups through to large cappuccino cups, depending on how big you like your coffee.
★ An etching tool – you can use anything to etch, such as the handle of a teaspoon, a bradawl (woodworking tool), cocktail stick or a skewer.
★ A damp cloth – for wiping your etching tool clean between etches.
★ Powdered food colouring – for colouring milk foam.
★ Thick card and a scalpel – to create stencil designs on top of your coffee art.

Steaming and Frothing Milk

You will need to steam and froth milk to pour into an espresso to create the base (see right). The foam texture should be velvety. The amount of milk foam you need depends on what size of cup you are using. For a 300ml (10fl oz) cup you will need 235ml (8½fl oz) of cold milk. The milk should be frothed and steamed to about 60°C (140°F), unless you are making a babyccino, in which case it should be no hotter than 50°C (122°F).

What is the 'crema'?

A combination of 'crema' and milk foam is needed to create latte art. The 'crema' is the velvety chocolate-coloured layer of espresso that naturally forms on top as the coffee is poured. The art of creating a design through pouring relies on maintaining the crema as a contrast to the white milk foam. Simply pouring milk into a coffee without following the basic steps below will destroy the crema and leave you with no pattern on top of your coffee.

Creating the Base

As you pour your base, your main focus should be to keep the crema on top at all times.

Pour an espresso into any size of cup (we have used a 300ml /10fl oz cup). Hold the cup with the handle facing your body and tilt the cup 45 degrees.

Pour the steamed milk into the middle of the coffee from a height of about 8cm (3 inches). The milk will go into the espresso, but the crema will stay on the top to create a layer of soft froth.

Pour in a consistent stream, zigzagging the flow of milk across the cup, left to right and back again, as if you are drawing smiles across the cup as it fills up. This will maintain the crema.

As you pour, lower the jug closer to the cup until the cup is two-thirds full (or as full as the recipe specifies). Create your design as instructed.

Dhan's Top Tips

★ Support the forearm of your pouring hand with your other hand if this helps to keep it steady. Moving your wrist rather than your whole arm is also a good way to keep your pouring and etching steady.

★ Take a deep breath before you start to pour a design and slowly let it out as you pour – this will help you stay steady and focussed on the design.

★ I like to stand with a wide and firm stance so that I don't wobble while I'm pouring – this position has been nicknamed the 'Dhan Tamang Stand'.

★ 'Following the white' is the phrase used to explain how you should always ensure the flow of milk goes into the same hole created by the pouring.

★ Bang the cup on the work surface to get rid of any bubbles you see forming on the surface. This also works to level out foam if you're making 3D designs (see pages 88–103).

★ Remember to keep a damp cloth to hand to wipe your etching tool between each etch – especially if you are using coloured milk foam.

★ To make the milk foam for 3D designs you will need to froth the milk until it has doubled in size. You can then use the 'quenelle' technique (see page 95) to thicken and stiffen the milk foam enough to make shapes with.

Basic Designs
Heart

The heart is the easiest coffee art design and the first one baristas are taught. You'll no doubt be familiar with it already, as most coffee shops use the design.

1 Create your base (see page 7) in a coffee cup.

2 Once the cup is two-thirds full, drop the jug closer to the cup and pour into the side closest to you – this will begin to create the heart shape as a white circle will start to form on the surface and get larger as you pour.

3 Once the cup is almost full and you have created a large white circle of foam, raise the stream and draw a line of milk through the middle of the circle to create a heart shape.

Once you've mastered pouring a heart you can develop this into a tulip. The tulip is a basic but very pretty design and can itself be developed into more complex patterns.

Tulip

1 Create your base (see page 7) in a coffee cup. When the cup is around two-thirds full, stop pouring.

Keeping the cup at an angle, pour foam into the centre to create a small milk circle, then stop, drawing up slightly at the end to create a kind of heart shape.

2

3

4

Create another, slightly smaller, circle of milk above the first one, again bringing the jug up at the end to create the heart shape.

Pour a third, smaller, circle of milk above the second, but this time finish by lifting the jug and running the milk through the middle of all three circles to create your tulip.

Rosetta

The rosetta is probably the most common design in coffee shops today – it seems every barista pops a rosetta on a flat white or latte. Like the tulip and heart, the rosetta is an important design to master as it is used in many of the other designs in this book.

Create your base (see page 7) in a coffee cup.

Once the cup is two-thirds full, drop the jug closer to the cup and continue pouring to form a white circle on the surface. This will be the base of your rosetta. Now start wiggling the jug left to right as you pour.

3 As you continue to wiggle and pour, move the jug toward the edge of the cup. You should see the fronds of the rosetta starting to form.

When you near the edge of the cup, lift the jug to about 3cm (1 inch) away from the surface and finish with a line of milk through the middle of the design – this will create a strong-looking leaf

4

FREE POURING

Free pouring really is the basis of all coffee art designs, and by mastering this invaluable technique, you will be opening your coffee repertoire up to a wealth of possible creations. There are various degrees of difficulty to the designs within this chapter, starting with the fairly basic Double Heart (see page 16) through to the elegant Windmill (see page 25) and the abstract Winged Tulip design (see page 30). They require different levels of skill, but all the designs in this chapter use the three basic designs of the Heart (see page 9), Tulip (see page 10) and Rosetta (see page 12) as a starting point.

Free pouring is one of the best coffee art skills to start with as it only requires a minimal amount of equipment – a pouring jug, a coffee cup and some steamed milk. Having a steady hand will help you to achieve great results with these free pouring designs. Practise, practise and practise again, before moving on to the more complex designs. It is often useful to have a few practise runs to try out the different elements of a design before putting them all together too.

Let the designs in this chapter inspire your imagination and creativity and see what other patterns and artworks you can make using the basic free pouring skills.

Double Heart

The secret of this beautifully simple pattern is to create a heart within a heart. This is done by pouring two hearts, one on top of the other. As you pour, the second heart pushes the outline of the first to the edge, resulting in concentric hearts.

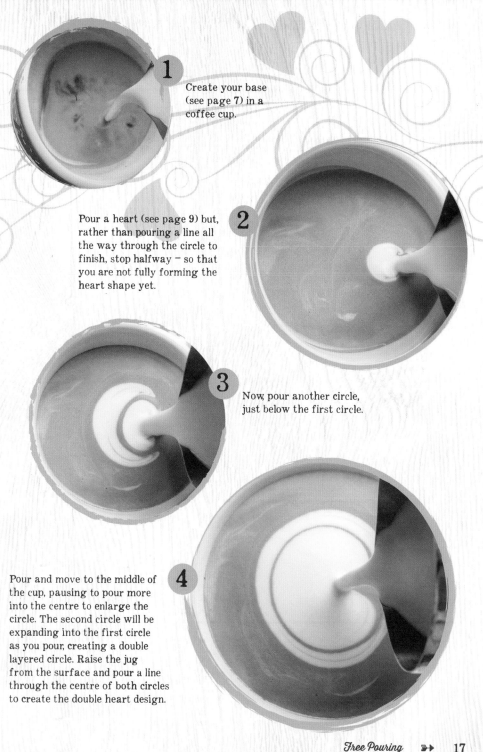

1 Create your base (see page 7) in a coffee cup.

Pour a heart (see page 9) but, rather than pouring a line all the way through the circle to finish, stop halfway – so that you are not fully forming the heart shape yet. **2**

3 Now, pour another circle, just below the first circle.

Pour and move to the middle of the cup, pausing to pour more into the centre to enlarge the circle. The second circle will be expanding into the first circle as you pour, creating a double layered circle. Raise the jug from the surface and pour a line through the centre of both circles to create the double heart design. **4**

This is a simple tulip design (see page 10) with added layers, so it's best to get your tulip technique perfected before attempting this more elaborate design. The key to achieving the extra layers is to start the tulip sooner in the pouring process, so don't fill the cup too full before beginning your design.

(see page 10)

TIP

You can do as many layers as you like — my best so far is 17 layers in an espresso cup!

Multi-layered Tulip

1 Create your base (see page 7) in a coffee cup, but stop pouring when your cup is one-third full.

2 Keeping the cup at an angle, pour your first circle into the centre of the cup as for the basic tulip design (see page 10).

3 Start the second circle slightly below the first, moving the stream of milk up as you pour to push the circle higher in the cup.

4 Continue to pour layers beneath one another until you reach the bottom side of the cup, making them smaller each time.

Finish by raising the jug and drawing a line through the middle of all the circles to create a multi-layered tulip.

5

This design is a combination of the tulip (see page 10) and heart (see page 9) patterns. Once you've mastered these basic designs, take it a step further to create this elegant swan pattern.

Swan ⟶

1

Create your base (see page 7) in a coffee cup, but stop pouring when your cup is one-third full.

2

Pour a five-layered tulip (see page 18) making all the circles slightly smaller than in the basic design.

3

When you get to the final circle, make it a little bigger than the previous one and then, continuing to pour, bring the jug diagonally down one side of the layers to create the back of the swan.

Bring the stream of milk back up so that it is running adjacent to the circles, up to the level of the final circle, to create the neck of the swan. Once you are level with the final circle, draw a small circle and pour through the centre to create a heart for the swan's head and beak.

4

Inverted Tulip

This is another tulip design, but this time we will be creating two tulips sitting against one another. The key is to twist the cup so you can make two tulips back to back.

Create your base (see page 7) in a coffee cup but hold the cup with the handle facing away from your body this time, and pour until the cup is one-third full.

1

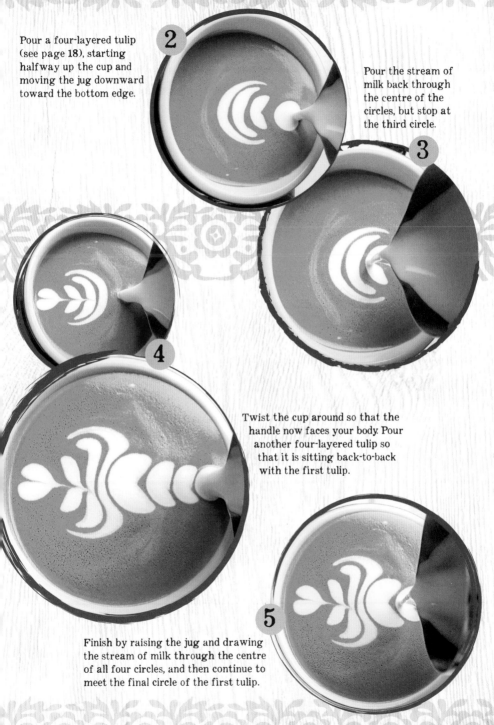

Pour a four-layered tulip (see page 18), starting halfway up the cup and moving the jug downward toward the bottom edge.

2

Pour the stream of milk back through the centre of the circles, but stop at the third circle.

3

4

Twist the cup around so that the handle now faces your body. Pour another four-layered tulip so that it is sitting back-to-back with the first tulip.

5

Finish by raising the jug and drawing the stream of milk through the centre of all four circles, and then continue to meet the final circle of the first tulip.

Up until now the cup has been fairly static, while the jug does all the movement. However, for this simple but effective design, the cup needs to rotate as you make the tulip designs around the edge.

Vortex Tulip

1 Create your base (see page 7) in a coffee cup and pour until the cup is half full.

2 Starting at the edge of the cup, pour a series of circles as for the basic tulip (see page 10) but, as you pour the circles, one below the other, twist the cup so the petals of the tulip sit around the outside edge of the cup.

3 Pour seven circles in total, getting smaller each time, and finish by raising the jug and pouring the stream of milk back round through the centres of the circles.

The

Windmill

Create your base (see page 7) in a coffee cup and pour until the cup is half full.

1

2

Starting at the edge of the cup, pour a series of circles as for the basic tulip (see page 10) but, as you pour the circles, one below the other, twist the cup so the petals of the tulip sit around the outside edge of the cup – pour as many as you need to go all the way round the cup (I have poured eight here).

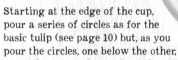

3

Keep pouring consistently, with the same rate of flow, so that the weight of the milk drops deep into the coffee and draws the circles into the centre – this will create the windmill pattern.

4

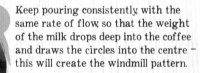

Stop pouring, then move to the middle of the cup and start another pour in the centre, swiftly raising the jug upward so that you have a gap of about 15cm (6 inches) between the jug and the coffee.

Tulip in a Pot

This is a lovely way to combine two basic patterns by using half of the tulip to create a rosetta and the other to create the tulip. Although it is a simple design, it won me the 2013 UK Latte Art Championship – my first award!

TIP

It's important to create the rosetta first as you won't get the same level of detail if you do it the other way around.

Create your base (see page 7) in a coffee cup but hold the cup with the handle facing away from your body this time, and pour until the cup is half full.

1

2 Create a rosetta (see page 12) toward the right-hand side of the cup. Don't draw the line through the middle.

3 Stop pouring and turn the cup 180 degrees, so the handle is now facing toward you. Pour a four-layered tulip design (see page 18) from the base of the rosetta (so that they sit back to back). The first circle of the tulip will push out the bottom of the rosetta.

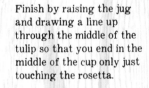

Finish by raising the jug and drawing a line up through the middle of the tulip so that you end in the middle of the cup only just touching the rosetta.

4

Flapping Swan

This is the first design that combines all three basic designs: tulip, rosetta and heart. It's a round design that fills the cup nicely.

VARIATION

See page 50 for ideas on how to use an etching tool to convert your flapping swan into a phoenix, rising from the flames!

1 Create your base (see page 7) in a coffee cup and pour until the cup is half full.

2 Start in the middle as if you were creating a double heart (see page 16), but on this occasion, make three circles, pushing each one down as you go. This will create three circles within one another.

3 From the top edge of the three-layered heart create a small rosetta (see page 12) moving up toward the top left of the cup, finishing at about 2 o'clock. Pour along the side of the rosetta rather than through the middle to finish this part of the design.

4 Pour another rosetta from the bottom edge of the circle, finishing at about 4 o'clock, and finish along the side again (rather than through the middle).

5 Still working with the jug close to the surface, pour a circle in between the two rosettas, close to the heart. Keep pouring and move up toward the right-hand side of the cup, lifting the jug as you do, to create the neck of the bird. Finish by pouring a small circle at the end of the neck and flick up through the middle to make a heart for the head.

Winged Tulip

This is a beautiful abstract design which nicely combines rosettas with a tulip to create an intricate pattern. You really need to concentrate on the detail of the wing to create the best design.

TIP
The more you wriggle the jug the more detailed the wing will be.

1 Create your base (see page 7) in a coffee cup and pour until the cup is half full.

2

To create the wing, pour a rosetta (see page 12) starting in the centre of the cup and moving to the right. Wiggle the jug and push the rosetta to the left as you pour and finish about halfway across the cup by pouring through the centre of the rosetta.

3

Next pour a tulip (see page 10), starting in the centre of the cup, just underneath the rosetta. Add as many layers to the tulip as you like (or can fit in). As you pour, you will be pushing the tulip into the rosetta so that the rosetta spreads out around the tulip to form the wings.

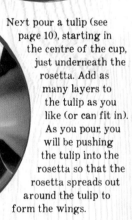

4 Raise the jug and pour through the centre of the tulip to finish.

Slosetta

This is effectively a very slowly (or lazily) poured rosetta. You may think this looks like a novice trying to pour a rosetta, but in fact it takes a steady hand to make a slosetta look impressive.

TIP

It's important to keep your hand steady and the pattern slow so that the lines become a lot thicker than the normal rosetta.

Create your base (see page 7) in a coffee cup and pour until the cup is half full.

Starting at the top of the cup, pour a rosetta (see page 12), but now instead of wiggling the jug, draw slow loops from left to right, narrowing as you move down the cup.

When you reach the bottom of the cup, pause briefly to create a circle at the top of the slosetta.

Pour a line through the centre of the circle and then all the way through the design to finish.

Once you have mastered the slosetta,
you should be able to take on this
effective bunch of grapes design.

Grapevine

1 Create your base (see page 7) in a coffee cup and pour until the cup is half full. Turn the cup so the handle is facing away from you.

2 Starting at the 7 o'clock position, pour a small slosetta (see page 32) of around four swirls moving down the side of the cup.

3 Pour a line through the middle and continue to pour in an arc over to the other side of the cup to create the impression of a vine.

4 Bring the jug closer to the coffee and draw a thick line of about 4cm (1½ inches) at the base of the vine.

Pour small unfinished hearts underneath the thick line for the grapes. You can add as many as you like, but I've simply done six circles here to create the impression of a bunch.

5

Wave Heart

This is a beautiful design with an innovative technique which relies upon creating movement in the base coffee. This develops the pattern around the edge of the cup.

Create your base (see page 7) in a coffee cup, but this time move the jug in a small circular motion as you pour (rather than side to side). This will start to swirl the coffee. Don't move too quickly, otherwise the design will spread out too much — you just need a slight movement. Pour until the cup is half full.

2 Once the base is moving to your satisfaction, pause at the bottom edge of the cup, keep pouring the milk, then start to wiggle the jug. This will create a pattern that will move forward around the cup. If the swirl is not moving fast enough you can move the jug back to help with the length of the pattern.

3 As the pattern goes around the outside of the cup, make the wiggles shorter so the pattern gets narrower.

Once the pattern goes three-quarters of the way around the edge of the cup, bring the stream of milk into the centre and bring the jug close to the coffee.

Pour a heart and finish it by flicking the stream back toward the edge of the cup, raising the jug as you move to make a delicate point.

FREE POURING

AND

ETCHING

Latte art really is an art, and where free pouring can only take you so far, the technique of etching will allow you to add more detail and interesting elements to your designs. By combining free pouring with etching, a whole world of coffee designs opens up. On your coffee canvas you could create a Tudor rose (see page 40), a beautiful phoenix (see page 50), a Mexican man (see page 54) or even a surfer cresting a wave (see page 70)... all in your coffee cup!

You can use a variety of different tools for etching, from a skewer to a bradawl to a cocktail stick to a modelling tool. In some instances, you will need a finer point for tiny detail than at other times. I mostly use a bradawl, which is a woodworking tool, resembling a small screwdriver. Whatever you use, always make sure you have a damp cloth to hand so that you can clean the point of your tool after each bit of etching.

I also introduce my trademark use of colour in this chapter. Adding colour to steamed milk will add another dimension to your designs and can help to create real showstoppers. Simply mix about 2g (½ teaspoon) of powdered food colouring with 20ml (4 teaspoons) steamed milk in a coffee cup. Stir thoroughly to combine and use this coloured milk to add detail to your designs, or add it to your jug of steamed milk to create a coloured pattern as you pour.

Tudor Rose

This is a simple etching to start you off. There isn't a great deal of work involved, but it is a swift way to achieve an impressive design.

1 First pour a little milk foam into a small espresso cup to be used later. Next, take a larger coffee cup and create your base (see page 7), pouring the milk until your cup is full. Set the coffee cup on the table in front of you with the handle pointing to the right.

Use the handle end of a teaspoon to take some of the reserved milk foam and place a small spot in the middle of the cup.

2

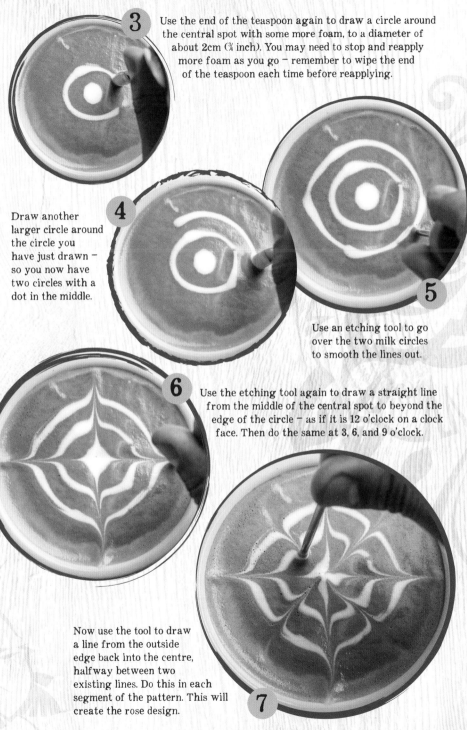

3 Use the end of the teaspoon again to draw a circle around the central spot with some more foam, to a diameter of about 2cm (¾ inch). You may need to stop and reapply more foam as you go – remember to wipe the end of the teaspoon each time before reapplying.

Draw another larger circle around the circle you have just drawn – so you now have two circles with a dot in the middle.

4

5

Use an etching tool to go over the two milk circles to smooth the lines out.

6 Use the etching tool again to draw a straight line from the middle of the central spot to beyond the edge of the circle – as if it is 12 o'clock on a clock face. Then do the same at 3, 6, and 9 o'clock.

Now use the tool to draw a line from the outside edge back into the centre, halfway between two existing lines. Do this in each segment of the pattern. This will create the rose design.

7

This design follows on from the Tudor Rose (see page 40), but involves etching using the coffee base itself. You can decorate the body and wings of the butterfly with as much or as little detail as you wish – just let your imagination be your guide.

Butterfly

1 First pour a little milk foam into a small espresso cup to be used later. Next, take a larger coffee cup and, with the handle facing away from you, create your base (see page 7), pouring until the cup is two-thirds full. Set the cup on the table in front of you with the handle pointing to the right.

Start by creating a triple heart in the centre of the cup as instructed with the Double Heart on page 16, but with an extra circle. Don't finish the design though, just move the pour slightly back into the centre and stop so the heart has a circular bottom.

2

3

Use an etching tool to draw from the centre of the circle toward 11 o'clock, then again toward 1 o'clock – this will make the tops of the wings.

4 Draw two lines, close together at the base of the circle, from the outside edge into the centre, to create the base of the abdomen.

5 Now draw two lines from the centre of the circle to the edge of the cup, one at 5 o'clock and one at 7 o'clock.

6 To create a segment in each wing, draw from the outside of the butterfly toward the centre on one side at about 4 o'clock and the other at about 8 o'clock, curving the line round and down a little as you go.

7 Pick up some of the darker coffee from the edge of the cup with the etching tool and draw the rest of the abdomen, moving from the two lines at the base of the circle, up through the middle to the top.

8 Use the reserved foam to draw two spots at the top of the cup, then draw lines down to the top of the body to make the antennae. Use another spot of foam for the head.

9 Now you can decorate the butterfly by dabbing into the darker coffee with the etching tool and using it to draw the spots on the wings and the eyes.

The rabbit is a fun design that uses a big heart to fake the effect of the ears.

Bunny Rabbit

1 Start by creating your base (see page 7) and pour until your cup is two-thirds full. Set the coffee cup on the table in front of you with the handle pointing to the right.

Hold the jug close to the surface of the coffee and create a heart (see page 9) just off centre. As you finish the heart by moving the pour through the centre, keep pouring slowly while moving the jug across the heart into the centre to create the head – this movement will elongate the heart so that you are left with a circular head and two rabbit ears.

2

3

When you are happy with the size of the bunny's head, set down the milk jug and use an etching tool to pick up some of the darker coffee from the edge of the cup and create the detail. It's best to draw the mouth first and then add the nose afterward.

4

Use the etching tool to add eyes, whiskers and detail on the ears.

5

Add a spot of milk on the eyes and nose for extra character.

Bear

→

Another cute animal creation, this is a fun and simple design with an impressive outcome. This pattern uses the tulip design as a base.

1 First pour a little milk foam into a small espresso cup to be used later. Next, take a larger coffee cup and, with the handle facing away from you, create your base (see page 7), pouring until the cup is two-thirds full.

2 Hold the jug close to the coffee surface and pour an unfinished tulip with two layers (see page 10).

3 Set the coffee cup on the table in front of you with the handle pointing to the right so the tulip is now upside down in front of you. Use the handle end of a teaspoon to pick up some of the reserved foam and make two blobs at the base of the cup for the paws.

4 Add two more blobs on top of the larger circle for the ears.

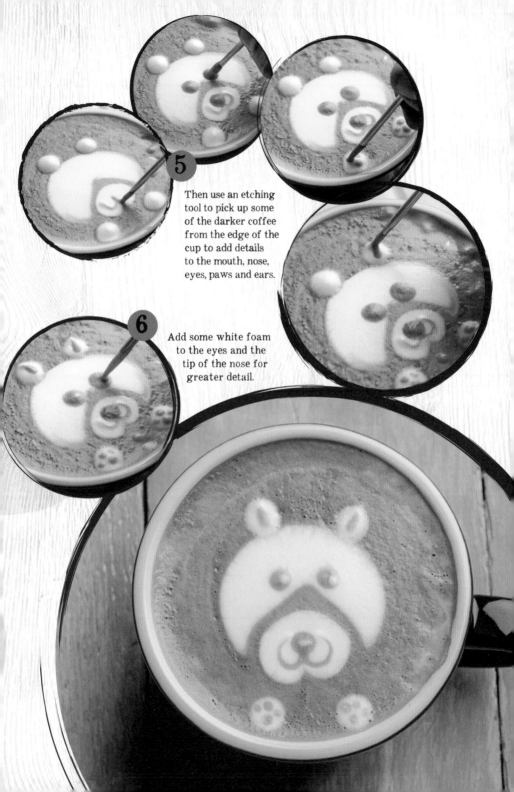

5

Then use an etching tool to pick up some of the darker coffee from the edge of the cup to add details to the mouth, nose, eyes, paws and ears.

6

Add some white foam to the eyes and the tip of the nose for greater detail.

This animal creation is based on the basic rosetta design. Again, the beauty is in the details you add with the etching tool, so see where your imagination takes you. I sometimes like to add colour to this design too.

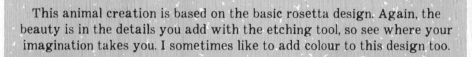

Elephant

First pour a little milk foam into a small espresso cup to be used later. Next, take a larger coffee cup and, with the handle facing away from you, create your base (see page 7), pouring until the cup is two-thirds full.

1

2 Pour a rosetta (see page 12), but instead of finishing it off by dragging a line back though the middle, curve the stream of milk slightly to the right to create a little flick and tilt the jug further into the cup to do a short, deep pour for the end of the elephant's trunk.

3 Set the coffee cup on the table in front of you with the handle pointing to the right – you should now have the elephant's face and trunk facing you. Use an etching tool to pick up some of the darker coffee at the edge of the cup and add two nostril holes on the end of the trunk.

4 Use the reserved foam to drag down two tusks on either side of the face.

5 Still using the foam, draw in ears at either side of the head by dragging lines up toward 11 o'clock and 1 o'clock and move them around and down to form large, floppy ears.

6 Use the darker coffee at the edge of the cup to add in eyes (and eyebrows if you like) and a row of dots down the centre of the forehead as jewels.

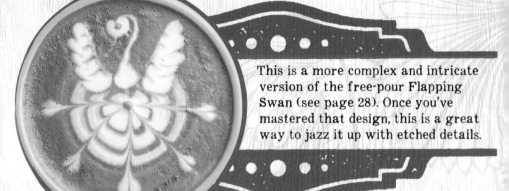

This is a more complex and intricate version of the free-pour Flapping Swan (see page 28). Once you've mastered that design, this is a great way to jazz it up with etched details.

Phoenix

1 First pour a little milk foam into a small espresso cup to be used later. Next, take a larger coffee cup and create the Flapping Swan design as instructed on page 28.

2 Set the coffee cup on the table in front of you with the handle pointing to the right – so the phoenix is now facing you. Use the handle end of a teaspoon and the reserved foam to dab five blobs around the bottom of the cup. Start with the blob directly below the phoenix's head, then move on to the top right one, then top left one, then the two blobs in between – this will help you space the blobs evenly.

3

Use an etching tool to drag a line from each blob into the centre of the concentric hearts. Pick up some of the darker coffee at the edge of the cup to mark where all of these dragged lines join with a blob of darker coffee.

4

To finish your design, use the etching tool to add an eye to the phoenix's head.

VARIATION

★ You can take this design further by adding a comb on top of the phoenix's head. Dot little blobs of foam in a line on top of the head and drag through them.
★ You can also drag more lines through the concentric hearts to create a more intricate design.
★ Carry on adding details until you're happy with the finished design.

Native American Chief

This design involves more drawing than pouring, so let your creative spirit run wild! It is based on the rosetta design (see page 12), and is a real crowd-pleaser, which can be embellished as much or as little as you like.

TIP

You can add your own personal touch to this design by adding wrinkles, a pipe, or anything else you fancy.

1 First pour a little milk foam into a small espresso cup to be used later. Next, take a larger coffee cup and, with the handle facing away from you, create your base (see page 7) and fill your cup to two-thirds full.

2 Create a rosetta (see page 12), starting right of centre. Instead of finishing it through the middle, pour up and left, circling around to create a loop that will become the chief's face.

3 Set the coffee cup on the table in front of you with the handle pointing to the right – so the chief's face is now facing you. Fill in the loop of the face by gently spooning on some of the reserved foam.

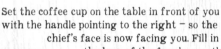

4 Draw a small line with the etching tool about halfway down the face, moving in toward the centre to create a line of darker coffee for the base of the nose. Create the mouth in the same way by drawing another line halfway between the base of the nose and the bottom of the face.

5 Run the etching tool lightly around the edge of the face to neaten the edges and create a cleaner line.

Pick up some of the darker coffee from the edge of the cup with the etching tool and draw an eyebrow and eye halfway between the top of the nose and the hair.

6

7 Use the same technique to draw a headband along the top and side of the face and decorate as you wish.

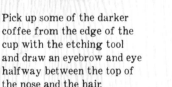

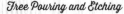

Mexican Man

This is one of my earliest designs; it's one that seems to suddenly appear on the surface of the coffee from a couple of carefully placed simpler designs.

1

Hold your cup with the handle facing toward you. Start by creating your base (see page 7) and fill your cup to two-thirds full.

2

Pour one layer of an unfinished tulip (see page 10), and then immediately pour an unfinished rosetta (see page 12) on top of it to create the hat, but don't drag the finishing lines through either of these two designs.

3

Turn the cup 180 degrees so the handle now faces away from you. Pour one large unfinished heart (a large circle) underneath the hat to make the face, keeping the jug close to the surface of the coffee.

4 Use the darker coffee at the edge of the cup and an etching tool to add in more detail. Start by adding a moustache by dragging two lines out and down from the centre of the face.

5 Next, draw a mouth, eyebrows, eyes, a nose and any other facial details you'd like.

Dragonfly

This is a charming design which works just as well with etching as without. You can add as much or as little detail as you'd like – I like to add antennae and decorate the wings, but not too much as the simplicity of the design is what makes it.

1 First pour a little milk foam into a small espresso cup to be used later. Next, take a larger coffee cup and, with the handle facing toward you, create your base (see page 7) and fill your cup to two-thirds full.

2 From the very centre of the cup, pour two loops of a slosetta (see page 32) on one side of the cup to form one set of wings. Take this slowly – you only need two loops on each side.

3 Mirror this first set of wings on the other side of the cup so you have an even and symmetrical image. Make sure you leave a small gap (2cm/ ¾ inch) between the sets of wings.

4

Starting about 1cm (½ inch) from the bottom edge of the cup, draw a thin rosetta (see page 12) through the centre of the two sets of wings, ending in the centre of the cup. Don't finish the rosetta; instead, lift the jug up and pour two little tulip layers to create the abdomen and the head, which should pop out above the top of the wings.

With the pouring done, you can now add in some etched details. Use the reserved foam to add dots along each wing and antennae to the top of the head.

5

6

Use darker coffee from the edge of the cup to add eyes to the head to give it some character if liked.

Jumping Dolphin

Now you are ready to create a complete scene from latte art. This tropical tableau shows a dolphin leaping out of the water next to a palm-lined beach.

1 First pour a little milk foam into a small espresso cup to be used later. Next, take a larger coffee cup and, with the handle facing away from you, create your base (see page 7) and half-fill the cup.

Create an unfinished heart (see page 9) just below the centre of the cup. Next, draw the palm tree. Turn the cup so the handle is at 3 o'clock and pour a small unfinished rosetta (see page 12) close to the top edge of the cup, on the opposite side to the heart.

2

3 Turn the cup so the handle is now positioned at 11 o'clock and pour a second small unfinished rosetta starting at the same point as the first rosetta, but moving in the opposite direction.

4 Create a third unfinished rosetta starting from the point where the two small rosettas meet, moving at an angle toward the right and finishing at the 4 o'clock position.

5 Use an etching tool dipped into the reserved milk foam to drag each side of the unfinished heart outward. Place the tool in the centre of the heart and move it out to the side and beyond to elongate the edges and create the dolphin shape. Give the dolphin a spout too.

6 Use darker coffee from the edge of the cup to give the dolphin a nose and a tail, an eye and a side fin using the etching tool to create detail.

Draw some waves with the reserved foam beneath the dolphin.

7

8 Add some dots of foam under the palm tree branches for coconuts.

9 Finish your design by drawing some bubbles coming out of your dolphin's mouth.

Coloured Roses

Get ready to elevate your latte art skills to the next level by bringing colour into the mix. This design doesn't contain coffee, just steamed milk and food colouring.

1 First pour 20ml (4 teaspoons) steamed milk into a small espresso cup and colour it with 2g (½ teaspoon) red food colouring. Next, take a larger coffee cup and, with the handle facing toward you, create your base (see page 7), using the red-coloured milk as your espresso and pouring in uncoloured milk until your cup is two-thirds full.

2 To create the rose, first draw the flower. With the handle facing toward you, slowly draw a partial looped slosetta (see page 32) with two loops, holding the jug close to the cup to form thick lines.

3 Add three closely placed unfinished hearts above the slosetta – two side-by-side, and one almost pushing into the middle of the first two.

4 Turn the cup so the handle is positioned at 3 o'clock and, pouring from a distance, create a rosetta (see page 12) close to the bottom edge of the cup.

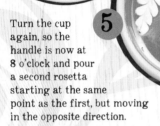

Turn the cup again, so the handle is now at 8 o'clock and pour a second rosetta starting at the same point as the first, but moving in the opposite direction.

5

6

To create the leaves, slowly draw two more partial looped slosettas, one above each rosetta, again holding the jug close to the cup to form thick lines. Continue the pour down in between the two rosettas and pour a small heart.

7 Turn the cup so the handle is now facing 3 o'clock. Drag an etching tool through the hearts at the top of the cup to create the petals of the rose.

9

Finally, draw a stalk, by dragging some of the white foam from the base of the rose down through the centre of the leaves and finishing at the rosettas – this will link all the elements of the design together.

8

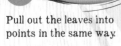

Pull out the leaves into points in the same way.

This beautiful design was created exclusively for the book and requires some free pouring and some etching, resulting in an ethereal scene.

Angel AND Cherry Tree

1 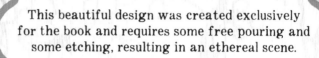 Prepare five espresso cups of milk foam in white, green, yellow, red and blue, following the instructions on page 60. Next, take a larger coffee cup and, with the handle facing toward you, create your base (see page 7) and fill your cup four-fifths full.

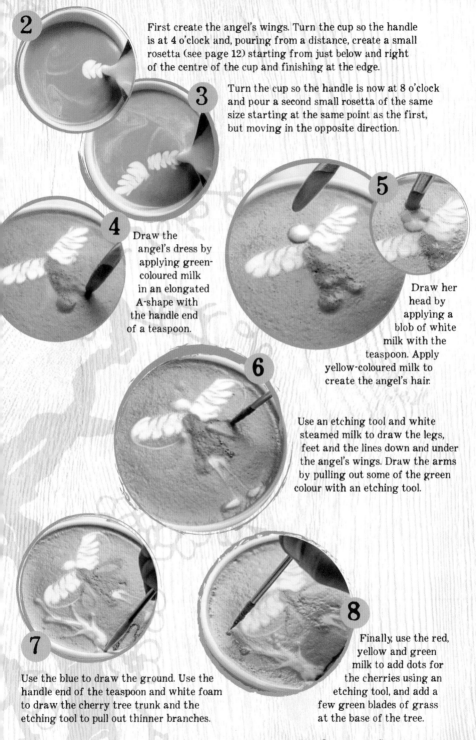

2 First create the angel's wings. Turn the cup so the handle is at 4 o'clock and, pouring from a distance, create a small rosetta (see page 12) starting from just below and right of the centre of the cup and finishing at the edge.

3 Turn the cup so the handle is now at 8 o'clock and pour a second small rosetta of the same size starting at the same point as the first, but moving in the opposite direction.

4 Draw the angel's dress by applying green-coloured milk in an elongated A-shape with the handle end of a teaspoon.

5 Draw her head by applying a blob of white milk with the teaspoon. Apply yellow-coloured milk to create the angel's hair.

6 Use an etching tool and white steamed milk to draw the legs, feet and the lines down and under the angel's wings. Draw the arms by pulling out some of the green colour with an etching tool.

7 Use the blue to draw the ground. Use the handle end of the teaspoon and white foam to draw the cherry tree trunk and the etching tool to pull out thinner branches.

8 Finally, use the red, yellow and green milk to add dots for the cherries using an etching tool, and add a few green blades of grass at the base of the tree.

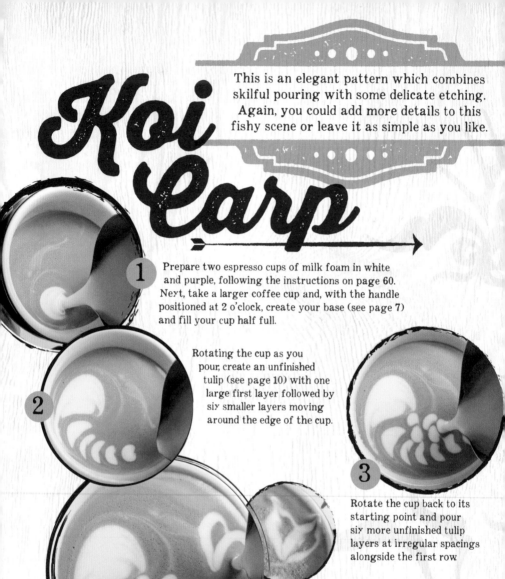

Koi Carp

This is an elegant pattern which combines skilful pouring with some delicate etching. Again, you could add more details to this fishy scene or leave it as simple as you like.

1 Prepare two espresso cups of milk foam in white and purple, following the instructions on page 60. Next, take a larger coffee cup and, with the handle positioned at 2 o'clock, create your base (see page 7) and fill your cup half full.

2 Rotating the cup as you pour, create an unfinished tulip (see page 10) with one large first layer followed by six smaller layers moving around the edge of the cup.

3 Rotate the cup back to its starting point and pour six more unfinished tulip layers at irregular spacings alongside the first row

4 Pour a two-looped slosetta (see page 32) to create the fish's tail. Use an etching tool to pull out the end of each tail fin.

5 Use the etching tool to pull out some of the tulip layers to make a side fin and a back fin.

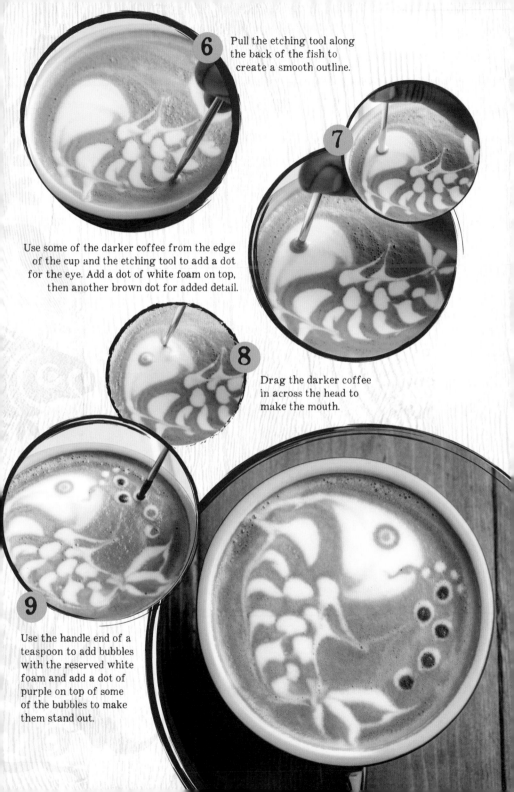

6 Pull the etching tool along the back of the fish to create a smooth outline.

7

Use some of the darker coffee from the edge of the cup and the etching tool to add a dot for the eye. Add a dot of white foam on top, then another brown dot for added detail.

8 Drag the darker coffee in across the head to make the mouth.

9 Use the handle end of a teaspoon to add bubbles with the reserved white foam and add a dot of purple on top of some of the bubbles to make them stand out.

This simple design looks much more challenging than it is. For the best contrast, use just milk without any coffee. This has the bonus of being suitable for children, who will love the colourful, mythical design.

The Unicorn

1 Prepare three espresso cups of milk foam in white, blue and red, following the instructions on page 60. Use a spoon to draw six horizontal lines of the red- and blue-coloured milks (alternating each colour) on the top of a jug of steamed milk.

2 Next, take a larger coffee cup and, with the handle facing away from you, fill the cup three-quarters full with uncoloured steamed milk. Then, using your coloured jug of steamed milk, create a basic rosetta (see page 12) off-centre in the cup to make the neck of the unicorn – the milk will pour in a coloured pattern.

When you reach the bottom of the cup, drag up to form a line at the edge of the neck, instead of pouring through the centre of the rosetta. Pour another smaller rosetta going off at an angle from the neck to create the head.

Dip an etching tool into one of the colours and zigzag a line to create the horn at the top of the head. Repeat with the other colour to create a spiral effect.

Use the etching tool to give the unicorn some stray hair by pulling colour from the top of its head. Add a blob of white milk foam for the eye and outline this with a single colour. Blob a contrasting colour in the centre to create the pupil.

Dip the etching tool into the white foam and give the unicorn a mouth. Add a blob of milk foam to the nose for a nostril. Finally, add an ear at the top of the head to complete the image.

Flamingo

This playful and colourful design is a great showstopper and looks more complex than it is. As with all of these designs, once you've mastered the basics (see pages 9, 10 and 12), anything is possible.

1 Prepare three espresso cups of milk foam in white, red and green, following the instructions on page 60. Next, take a larger coffee cup and, with the handle positioned at 3 o'clock, create your base (see page 7) and fill your cup three-quarters full.

2 Pour a rosetta (see page 12) starting from the centre, moving toward the handle and ending at the edge of the cup.

3 Pour three small unfinished tulip layers (see page 10) directly beneath the rosetta, for the flamingo's body.

4 Use the handle end of a teaspoon to position a blob of the reserved white foam at 12 o'clock to make the head.

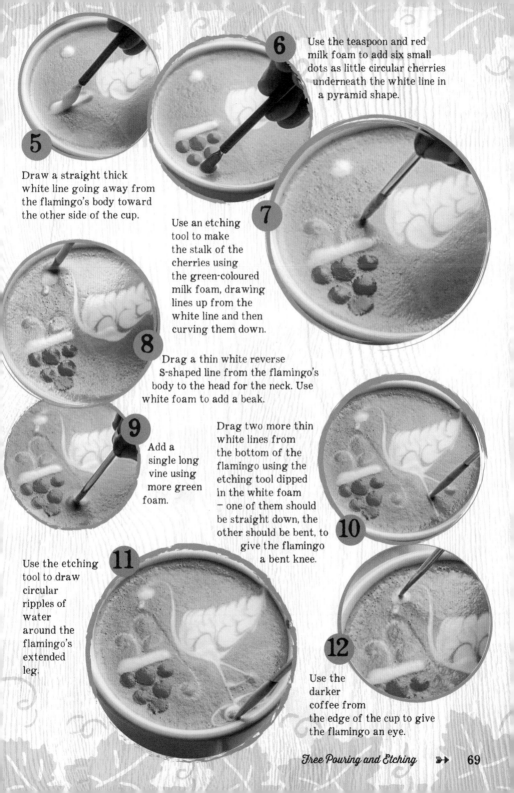

5

Draw a straight thick white line going away from the flamingo's body toward the other side of the cup.

6

Use the teaspoon and red milk foam to add six small dots as little circular cherries underneath the white line in a pyramid shape.

7

Use an etching tool to make the stalk of the cherries using the green-coloured milk foam, drawing lines up from the white line and then curving them down.

8

Drag a thin white reverse S-shaped line from the flamingo's body to the head for the neck. Use white foam to add a beak.

9

Add a single long vine using more green foam.

10

Drag two more thin white lines from the bottom of the flamingo using the etching tool dipped in the white foam – one of them should be straight down, the other should be bent, to give the flamingo a bent knee.

11

Use the etching tool to draw circular ripples of water around the flamingo's extended leg.

12

Use the darker coffee from the edge of the cup to give the flamingo an eye.

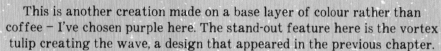

This is another creation made on a base layer of colour rather than coffee – I've chosen purple here. The stand-out feature here is the vortex tulip creating the wave, a design that appeared in the previous chapter.

Surfing Man

1

First pour a little milk foam into a small espresso cup to be used later. Next, pour 20ml (4 teaspoons) steamed milk into a larger coffee cup and colour it with 2g (½ teaspoon) purple food colouring. Now create your base (see page 7), pouring in the uncoloured steamed milk until your cup is half full.

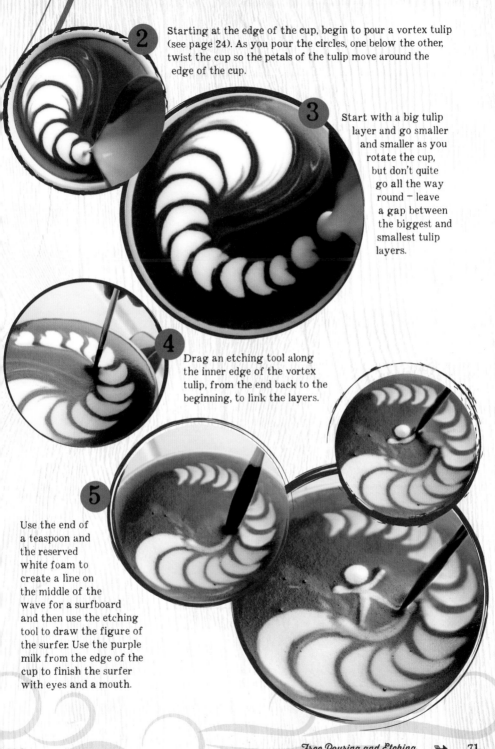

2 Starting at the edge of the cup, begin to pour a vortex tulip (see page 24). As you pour the circles, one below the other, twist the cup so the petals of the tulip move around the edge of the cup.

3 Start with a big tulip layer and go smaller and smaller as you rotate the cup, but don't quite go all the way round – leave a gap between the biggest and smallest tulip layers.

4 Drag an etching tool along the inner edge of the vortex tulip, from the end back to the beginning, to link the layers.

5 Use the end of a teaspoon and the reserved white foam to create a line on the middle of the wave for a surfboard and then use the etching tool to draw the figure of the surfer. Use the purple milk from the edge of the cup to finish the surfer with eyes and a mouth.

STENCILS

Using stencils will take your coffee art designs to another level of creativity. They are so versatile and can be as simple or as intricate as you'd like. The double heart design (see page 75) is a great place to start, before moving on to the more complex rose design (see page 79) and larger, more intricate scenes like the shark attack (see page 81) and swan lake (see page 82).

There are no real limits here, it just depends on your creative talent and how expressive you can be. Each design in this chapter comes with a stencil design to trace and cut out so that each artwork can be easily replicated. You will need some card that should be about 250gsm (10pt) in weight, but make sure it's not too thick that you can't cut out the designs. You will also need a scalpel and a cutting board. Simply trace or draw your design, cut it out, and then place the stencil on top of a poured coffee and sprinkle with chocolate powder. Remove the stencil to reveal your design.

Stencils are a great way to achieve some spectacular coffee art even if you are still unsure of your free pouring skills as it only requires a basic poured coffee plus the stencil design. Use the designs in this chapter as inspiration for creating any number of personalized artworks.

Coffee Bean

This simple yet effective design is very close to my heart and is the perfect choice for coffee lovers.

1 Trace the stencil on page **84** onto a piece of thick card and cut it out.

2 Pour a cappuccino with the jug held very close to the cup so that you create a central circle of white milk foam surrounded by a darker coffee-coloured ring. Leave some height between the coffee and the rim of the cup to ensure the stencil will rest on top without getting wet.

3 Put the coffee cup in front of you with the handle pointing to the right. Place the stencil on top of the coffee cup with the coffee bean shape sitting over the circle of white foam. Liberally sprinkle chocolate powder over the stencil, making sure the shape left beneath is sharp and the chocolate has gone all the way to the edges of the coffee bean.

4 Lift the stencil, taking care not to knock any excess chocolate over the surface of the cappuccino.

This is the perfect design to impress your loved one on Valentine's Day and works best on top of a cappuccino.

Two Hearts

1 Trace the stencil on page **84** onto a piece of thick card and cut it out.

Pour a cappuccino with the jug held very close to the cup so that you create a central circle of white milk foam surrounded by a darker coffee-coloured ring. Leave a little bit of height between the coffee and the rim of the cup to ensure the stencil will rest on top without getting wet. Put the coffee cup in front of you with the handle pointing to the right. Place the stencil on top of the coffee cup and liberally sprinkle chocolate powder over the stencil, making sure the shape left beneath is sharp and the chocolate has gone all the way to the edges of the heart.

2

3

Lift the stencil, shake off any excess chocolate, and flip it over, lining it up on top of the cup so the two hearts overlap. Sprinkle the chocolate again, this time more delicately to create a lighter heart. Remove the stencil and serve.

Star

Create a twinkly star to top your cappuccino with this simple design.

1

Trace the stencil on page 85 onto a piece of thick card and cut it out. Pour steamed milk into the cup. Make an espresso in a separate espresso cup. Now pour the espresso into the larger cup (it will go underneath the steamed milk foam, leaving a white layer of foam on the top).

2

Put the coffee cup in front of you with the handle pointing to the right. Place the stencil on top of the coffee cup and liberally sprinkle chocolate powder over the stencil, making sure the shape left beneath is sharp and the chocolate has gone all the way to the edges of the triangle.

3

Lift the stencil and rotate it to create a star shape. Sprinkle the chocolate again. Remove the stencil and serve.

Smiley Face

1 Trace the stencil on page 85 onto a piece of thick card and cut it out.

This cappuccino design will put a smile on any face.

2 Pour a cappuccino with the jug held very close to the cup so that you create a central circle of white milk foam surrounded by a darker coffee-coloured ring. Leave a little bit of height between the coffee and the rim of the cup to ensure the stencil will rest on top without getting wet.

3 Put the coffee cup in front of you with the handle pointing to the right. Place the stencil on top and liberally sprinkle chocolate powder over the stencil, making sure the shape left beneath is sharp and the chocolate has gone all the way to the edges of the smiley face. Remove the stencil and serve.

This elegant design is bound to wow your audience.

1

Trace the stencil on page 86 onto a piece of thick card and cut it out. Pour a cappuccino with the jug held very close to the cup so that you create a central circle of white milk foam surrounded by a darker coffee-coloured ring. Leave a little bit of height between the coffee and the rim of the cup to ensure the stencil will rest on top without getting wet.

2

Put the coffee cup in front of you with the handle pointing to the right. Place the stencil on top of the coffee cup and liberally sprinkle chocolate powder over the stencil, making sure the shape left beneath is sharp and the chocolate has gone all the way to the edges of the stag. Remove the stencil and serve.

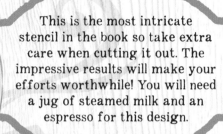

This is the most intricate stencil in the book so take extra care when cutting it out. The impressive results will make your efforts worthwhile! You will need a jug of steamed milk and an espresso for this design.

1 Trace the stencil on page 86 onto a piece of thick card and cut it out. Pour steamed milk into the cup. Make an espresso in a separate espresso cup. Now pour the espresso into the larger cup (it will go underneath the steamed milk foam, leaving a white layer of foam on top). Leave a little bit of height between the coffee and the rim of the cup to ensure the stencil will rest on top without getting wet.

2 Put the coffee cup in front of you with the handle pointing to the right. Place the stencil on top of the coffee cup and liberally sprinkle chocolate powder over the stencil, making sure the shape left beneath is sharp and the chocolate has gone all the way to the edges of the rose. Remove the stencil and serve.

Christmas Tree

You can embellish this simple stencil design using red- and green-coloured milk foam to decorate your tree with baubles.

1 Trace the stencil on page 87 onto a piece of thick card and cut it out. Prepare two espresso cups of milk foam in red and green, following the instructions on page 60. Pour a cappuccino with the jug held very close to the cup so that you create a central circle of white milk foam surrounded by a darker coffee-coloured ring. Leave a little bit of height between the coffee and the rim of the cup to ensure the stencil will rest on top without getting wet.

2 Put the coffee cup in front of you with the handle pointing to the right. Place the stencil on top of the coffee cup and liberally sprinkle chocolate powder over the stencil, making sure the shape left beneath is sharp and the chocolate has gone all the way to the edges of the Christmas tree. Remove the stencil.

3 Use the red- and green-coloured milk foams and the handle end of a teaspoon to add coloured baubles to the tree. Use an etching tool to attach the bauble to the tree.

Shark Attack

Make waves by using etching to embellish this scary stencil design. You will need a jug of steamed milk and an espresso.

1 Trace the stencil on page 87 onto a piece of thick card and cut it out. Pour steamed milk into a cup. Make an espresso in a separate espresso cup. Now pour the espresso into the larger cup – it will go underneath the steamed milk foam, leaving a white layer of foam on top. Leave a little bit of height between the coffee and the rim of the cup to ensure the stencil will rest on top without getting wet.

2 Prepare an espresso cup of milk foam in brown, following the instructions on page 60. Put the larger coffee cup in front of you with the handle pointing to the right. Place the stencil on top of the coffee cup and liberally sprinkle chocolate powder over the stencil, making sure the shape left beneath is sharp and the chocolate has gone all the way to the edges of the design.

3 Use an etching tool and brown milk foam to add waves beneath the design.

VARIATION
You could use blue-coloured steamed milk for the waves to add another element to this design.

Swan Lake

This design has maximum impact with minimum effort, and only takes a few seconds to create. It works best on top of a cappuccino.

1 Trace the stencil on page 87 onto a piece of thick card and cut it out.

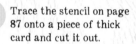

Pour steamed milk into a cup. Make an espresso in a separate espresso cup. Now pour the espresso into the larger cup – it will go underneath the steamed milk foam, leaving a white layer of foam on top. Leave a little bit of height between the coffee and the rim of the cup to ensure the stencil will rest on top without getting wet.

2

3 Put the coffee cup in front of you with the handle pointing to the right. Place the stencil over the coffee cup, lining up the base of the swan with the handle of the cup to create a horizontal 'water line'. Liberally sprinkle chocolate powder over the stencil, making sure the shape left beneath is sharp and the chocolate has gone all the way to the edges of the swan.

4 Lift the stencil, shake off any excess chocolate, and flip it over, lining it up so the two swans are exactly opposite each other across the 'water line' – like a reflection. Sprinkle the chocolate again, this time more delicately to create a lighter swan shape for the reflection in the lake.

5

Finish off the design by adding details such as plants on the surface of the water or try dragging your etching tool through the reflected swan to create ripples in the lake.

Stencil Templates

Trace the stencils onto a piece of thick card and cut them out.

Coffee Bean
page 74

Two Hearts
page 75

Star
page 76

Smiley
Face
page 77

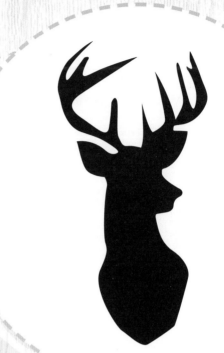

Stag
page 78

Rose
page 79

Swan Lake
page 82

Christmas Tree
page 80

Shark Attack
page 81

3D ART

Adding 3D designs to your creations adds a whole new dimension to coffee art. Who knew that a simple spoonful of frothed milk could add so much impact to a design? The simple act of frothing milk to create voluminous milk foam that can be moulded and shaped into a wealth of patterns and designs, will transform your coffee art from plain to exciting. In the same way as stencils, mastering the art of using these 3D designs is also great for anyone not comfortable with the free pouring and etching skills just yet.

3D designs are especially good when used on babyccinos as they are a fun way to get kids involved in coffee art. Coffee shops have realized that children want to mimic their parents by having a 'mini coffee', so babyccinos are just frothed milk in an espresso cup, making them the perfect basis for adding some great 3D designs. Cute animals such as a bear (see page 92), a family of bears (see page 91) or a pig (see page 94) are great designs, but really there are so many animals you can try.

This chapter also showcases some designs on top of poured coffees, but all of the designs in this chapter are suitable for making on top of a babyccino for kids too, especially the seasonal Santa Claus (see page 98), Easter Bunny (see page 99) and Hallowe'en scene (see page 100). Some of the 3D designs also use some etching and coloured milk to add more detail.

This is the easiest of the babyccino designs to create and is great for those starting out with foam creations. You will need a jug of steamed milk and some chocolate powder.

Babyccino Footprint

1

Fill a small coffee cup with steamed milk that is no hotter than 50°C (122°F) so it is cool enough for a child to drink. Froth some milk (it must be frothed and not just steamed) and set aside to use in a moment.

2 Tap the cup on the work surface to level the surface of the milk and then sprinkle a layer of chocolate powder on top of the foam. This will be the foundation for the 3D design and will stop the foam from sinking (and kids will love the extra chocolatey layer).

3 With the cup handle on the right-hand side, spoon a large blob of frothed milk foam into the centre of the cup at the bottom to create the pad of the footprint.

4 Add four smaller blobs for the toes above the larger blob.

VARIATION

To create a family of bears, prepare the espresso cup as above and prepare another cup of milk foam in brown. Use an etching tool and the brown milk foam to draw faces on each foam blob. I've also added a fifth bear peering over the side of the cup.

This variation on the basic footprint design creates a friendly babyccino bear.

Babyccino Bear

1 Fill a small coffee cup with steamed milk that is no hotter than 50°C (122°F) so it is cool enough for a child to drink. Froth some milk (it must be frothed and not just steamed) and set aside to use in a moment.

2 Tap the cup on the work surface to level the surface of the milk and then sprinkle a layer of chocolate on top of the foam to create the foundation for the 3D design.

3 With the cup handle on the right-hand side, spoon in a large blob of milk foam to create the head of the bear. Add two smaller blobs for the ears and another pair for the paws.

Now it's time to draw some features using an etching tool. You can either dip the etching tool directly into the chocolate layer at the side of the cup to create the details, or you could mix chocolate powder with some milk foam in an espresso cup and dip the etching tool into that (this way you will not make a mess of the chocolate at the edge of the cup). Give your bear a nose, mouth, eyes, ears and paw prints.

4

VARIATIONS

Elephant Babyccino – this variation on the Babyccino Bear is created by preparing the cup with milk foam and sprinkling with chocolate as above. Position the cup with the handle facing you. Add a large blob of milk at the base of the cup for the elephant's head and add two smaller blobs for ears on either side. Trail some milk foam down the handle of the cup for the trunk. Add detail with an etching tool and some chocolate.

Octopus Babyccino – this fun variation on the Babyccino Bear is created by preparing the cup with milk foam, sprinkling with chocolate and adding a large blob of foam for the octopus body as above. Then trail milk foam leading from the octopus's body to the edge of the cup and over the side for the tentacles. Use an etching tool and chocolate to add detail.

Babyccino Pig

This babyccino can also be made bigger on a cup of coffee, but it's more striking and lasts longer on milk and is easier to get the height in a small cup as you don't need so much foam.

Fill an espresso cup with steamed milk that is no hotter than 50°C (122°F) so it is cool enough for a child to drink. Froth some milk (it must be frothed and not just steamed), pour some of the milk foam into an espresso cup and add a little red food colouring to make pink-coloured foam.

1

2

Tap the first cup on the work surface to level the surface of the milk and then sprinkle a layer of chocolate powder on top of the foam to create the foundation for the 3D design.

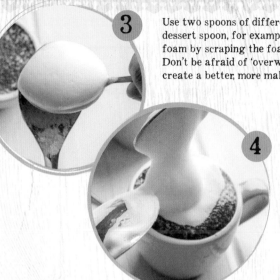

3 Use two spoons of different sizes (a teaspoon and dessert spoon, for example) to create a 'quenelle' of foam by scraping the foam from one spoon to another. Don't be afraid of 'overworking' the foam as it will create a better, more malleable consistency.

4 Place a large blob of the stiff foam in the centre of the cup to make the head of the pig. You will probably need at least one more spoonful placed directly on top to create a good height.

Place two smaller blobs of foam at the top of the 'head' for the ears, drawing the spoon upward to create the point of the ears. Add a smaller blob to create the nose and two more tiny blobs for the trotters.

5

6 Use an etching tool to paint the pink milk onto the nose, eyes, ears and trotters.

7

Pick up some of the chocolatey foam from the edge of the cup with the etching tool and paint the eyes and nostrils.

Cat Catching a Fish

This is a dynamic 3D design which extends over two cups – not one for the faint-hearted! Once perfected, this can be a real show-stopper.

TIP
Making a quenelle with the milk foam will stiffen and aerate the foam and make it stand taller and last longer in the design.

1 You will need two different-sized cups for this design – one espresso cup and one cappuccino cup. You will also need an espresso cup filled with milk foam mixed with chocolate powder to be used later. Pour an espresso coffee into each cup. Top up both cups with steamed milk to create a base (see page 7). Position the cups, just touching, with handles on the right-hand side and the espresso cup sitting in front of the cappuccino cup.

2 Use two spoons of different sizes (a teaspoon and dessert spoon) to create a 'quenelle' of foam by scraping the foam from one spoon to another. Start with the body of the cat. Drop blobs of the stiff foam onto the larger cup, starting at the edge touching the espresso cup. Drag the blob out into an oblong shape toward the opposite side of the cup. Keep adding the milk foam on top until you are happy with the shape and height of the body.

3 Next, with more stiffened milk, add two ears to the cat's body about 2cm (¾ inch) from the front edge of the cup. Create more stiffened foam with the quenelle method and add two paws on either side of the face of the cat. These should start at the rim of the cup and drop over the edge of the cup. The foam you use for this needs to be quite aerated and stiff so that it doesn't drop too quickly down the side of the cup.

Next, add a tail with more stiffened milk foam.

4

5

Drop two comma-shaped blobs of milk foam onto the surface of the espresso cup to create fish curling round each other in a circle.

6

Use an etching tool dipped in the chocolate milk foam to draw a nose and mouth onto the front of the cat's face. Add lines on either side for three whiskers and then two dots above for eyes.

8

Still using the chocolate milk and the etching tool, etch a few little lines on top of each of the cat's paws. Next, add some details to the fish in the espresso cup. Add eyes, a mouth and an outline to the fish. Add fins to the top and sides of the fish, along with tail fins.

7

Add two little triangles onto the ears and then a tuft of hair on the cat's head. Next, drag a line of chocolate down the back of the cat and add a few stripes across.

Santa Claus

This is a quick and easy-to-reproduce festive design that will really wow your family at Christmas-time.

1 Prepare three espresso cups of milk foam in red, white and brown, using chocolate powder to colour the brown one, following the instructions on page 60. Next, take a larger coffee cup and, with the handle facing away from you, create your base (see page 7) and fill your cup.

2 Use a teaspoon to create a tall triangle of white foam on the top of your base. You don't need to use the 'quenelle' method here, as this design doesn't need to stand out so much on top of the cup. Add a blob of foam at the top of the triangle to be the bobble on top of Santa's hat.

3 Use an etching tool dipped in the chocolate milk foam to draw an outline around the hat bobble and the edge of the triangle.

4 Draw the bottom of the hat and, just beneath that, Santa's eyes, eyebrows and nose. From the nose, draw two lines to make the moustache and extend to the edge of the cup to create the beard line. Now, use the etching tool and the red-coloured milk foam to colour the hat Christmas red.

VARIATION

I've used a coffee base here, but if you want to give this design to a child then you could make it on a steamed milk base with chocolate powder on top, or even on top of a hot chocolate for a treat.

Easter Bunny

1 Prepare three espresso cups of milk foam in red, white and brown, using chocolate powder to colour the brown one, following the instructions on page 60.

2 Hold a cappuccino cup with the handle facing away from you. Start by creating your base (see page 7) and fill your cup until it is full. Spoon a thick circle of white milk foam just off centre in the cup.

3 Next, using the 'quenelle' method (see page 95), add two blobs of stiffened foam to create the 3D ears at the top of the head.

4 Use an etching tool dipped in chocolate milk foam to draw in two eyes, a nose and a mouth. Next, add detail on the ears.

Add a blob of red foam to create a tongue under the mouth. Finish the rabbit with some whiskers.

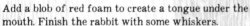

5

This Hallowe'en design creates a whole spooky scene on the surface of your coffee – a great seasonal artwork.

Hallowe'en

2 Spoon a circle of white milk foam just off centre in the cup to create the ghoulish face. Use the handle end of a teaspoon dipped in chocolate milk foam to outline the ground at the bottom of the mug and then fill it in.

1 Prepare three espresso cups of milk foam in red, white and brown, using chocolate powder to colour the brown one, following the instructions on page 60. Next, take a larger coffee cup and, with the handle facing away from you, create your base (see page 7) and fill your cup.

3 Draw a gnarled tree coming up from the ground and draw branches coming off it, with one coming across and above the white circle. Use an etching tool dipped in the chocolate milk foam to draw in some details, such as scorched branches poking out of the ground and bats in the air. Draw a chocolate rope coming down from the overhanging branch to suspend the white circle.

4 Use red coloured milk foam to draw a mouth at the bottom of the white circle and two eyes above the mouth. Use the etching tool to drag in little white teeth from the white foam surrounding the mouth. Finish off with two tiny dots of chocolate for the pupils.

This design relies on you mastering the 'quenelle' technique, to get the froth as stiff as you can so the mountains hold their shape even when built quite tall.

Mountain Range

TIP
It is worth working quickly with this design as the mountains will eventually succumb to gravity and flatten out.

1 Prepare an espresso cup of milk foam in brown, following the instructions on page 60. This design works best on a steamed milk base, so fill a cappuccino cup with steamed frothy milk. Tap the cup on the work surface to level the surface of the milk and then sprinkle a layer of chocolate on top.

2 Stiffen and thicken some milk froth using the 'quenelle' technique (see page 95). Drop a blob of stiffened froth onto the centre of the coffee cup. Repeat this step to create two more mountains on either side of the central one. You can use your spoons to shape and lift the mountains.

3 Drag a wavy line of white foam along the 'ground' in front of the mountains using the handle end of a teaspoon.

4 Finally, use an etching tool and brown milk foam to drag dark lines up the side of each mountain to give the impression of crevasses in the mountain side.

3D Flower

This design appears in this section of the book because of its use of foam as well as etching – the flower and leaves should be gently raised from the coffee's surface.

Prepare four espresso cups of milk foam in white, pink, green and brown, using chocolate powder to colour the brown one, following the instructions on page 60. Next, take a larger coffee cup and, with the handle facing away from you, create your base (see page 7) and fill your cup.

1

Use a teaspoon to pick up some white milk foam and add five dots in a circle to create the flower's head just off-centre, toward the side of the cup.

2

Use an etching tool to drag each blob outward to a point to create the petals.

3

4 Pick up some more white foam with the etching tool and dot it in the middle of the flower.

5

Still using the etching tool with white foam, draw the flower stem down toward the side of the cup closest to you. Draw two little leaf stems off this main stem in white.

6 Pick up some green-coloured milk foam with the handle end of a teaspoon and blob some green next to each leaf stem. Use the etching tool to drag the green blobs out to points to create the leaves.

7

Pick up some chocolate milk foam with the teaspoon handle and draw in a rib on each leaf and the ground underneath the plant. You can really embellish this as much as you want with more green foam – I've added some tufts of grass.

8 Pick up some pink-coloured milk foam on the end of the etching tool and add a dot of pink onto the white centre of the flower. Finally, draw a delicate pink oval inside each petal.

BLACK BELT BARISTA

These complex and technical designs aren't for the faint-hearted. Here we reveal the techniques behind some of my award-winning art for you to try at home. Some are difficult to master and require skill and patience, so practice really is your best friend here. I would advise really making sure you have mastered the basic designs and are confident with your pouring skills before trying these designs out. It is sometimes a good idea to practise each individual element of a design separately before you put them all together.

Most of the designs in this chapter have the addition of my signature use of colour and also etched details to take them to another level. I have won awards for some of these designs and they really do serve to showcase some of the best elements of coffee art.

As with all of the designs in this book, please do use these ideas as a starting point and feel free to go wherever your imagination and creativity takes you. With all of these designs, you can add as much or as little detail as you would like or feel comfortable with. Sometimes it's best to keep things simple, but other designs really benefit from extra etching to bring out details.

Owls

I premiered this design at the Shanghai 2016 World Latte Art Championships – it includes my signature use of colour and is a great design to move onto once you have mastered free pouring and etching.

1 Prepare four espresso cups of milk foam in white, yellow, red and green, following the instructions on page 60. Next, take a larger coffee cup and, with the handle facing away from you, create your base (see page 7) and fill your cup two-thirds full.

2 Pour four little rosettas (see page 12), from left to right, one under the other, with a gap between the first and second and the third and fourth rosettas. These are the wings of the two owls. Now set down your cup with the handle facing 3 o'clock. Use an etching tool to draw a line up the inside of each wing to smooth the edges.

3 Use the handle end of a teaspoon to add two blobs of white milk foam for the eyes above each set of wings. Add two smaller blobs of white milk foam under each set of wings for the feet.

4 Still using the teaspoon and white milk foam, draw a little crescent line under each owl. Then add a thinner line of white foam with the etching tool above each crescent line.

5 Use the handle end of the teaspoon and the yellow-coloured milk foam to draw a branch running underneath the owls.

Now use the etching tool and some white milk foam to outline the heads of the owls. Use a dot of white milk foam to form the beak of each owl and use the etching tool to pull each into a point. **6**

7 Use the handle end of the teaspoon to pick up some darker coffee from the edge of the cup and add dots to the eyes.

8 Use the etching tool to add a tiny dot of red foam for each pupil.

9 Use the etching tool and white milk foam to etch intermittent feathers down the chests of the owls. Then drag four vertical lines up through the crescents under each owl to turn them into little tail feathers.

10 Use red milk foam to add blobs onto the branches underneath the owls for berries. Then use green-coloured milk foam to etch leaves for the berries. Finally, use the etching tool to add white foam dots to each of the red berries to give them a reflective glint.

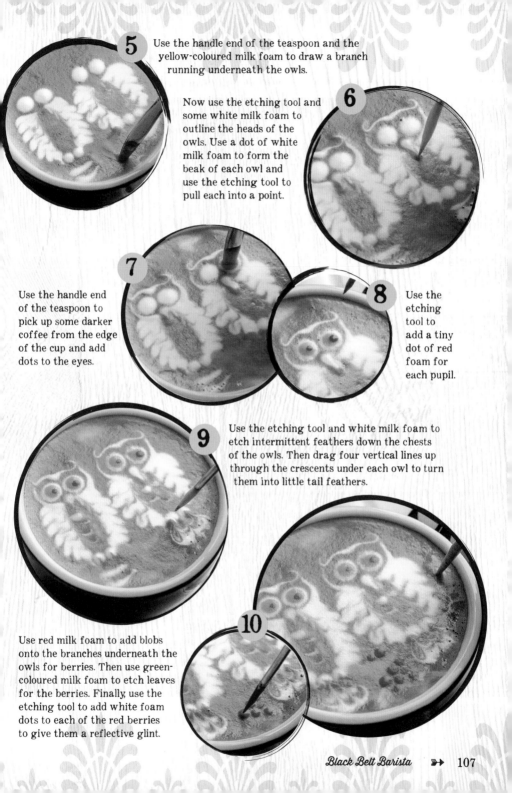

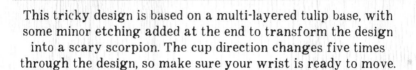

This tricky design is based on a multi-layered tulip base, with some minor etching added at the end to transform the design into a scary scorpion. The cup direction changes five times through the design, so make sure your wrist is ready to move.

Scorpion

1 Hold the cup with the handle facing away from you. Start by creating your base (see page 7) and fill your cup half full. Start in the middle of the cup and pour a three-layered tulip (see page 18).

2 Turn the cup so the handle is now facing you and pour three more unfinished tulip layers which push into the original three, distorting the circular shape.

3 Turn the cup again, back to the start position, and pour three more smaller unfinished tulip layers against the original ones you first poured. These will form the tail of the scorpion.

4 Turn the cup back round again so the handle is facing you and, at each side of the scorpion's body, add three small unfinished tulip layers which finish just at the edge of the cup. These form the pincers of the scorpion.

Once again, turn the cup around, this time so the handle points to 3 o'clock. Add six more little unfinished tulip layers to the end of the scorpion's tail, curling round the rim of the cup. Take a little longer over the last one and drag the stream of milk down to give the tail its point. **5**

6 Set the cup down gently, with the handle facing 3 o'clock, and grab an etching tool. Between the two pincers, drag two pointy lines down, into the head, to make a mouth for the scorpion.

7 Do the same thing at the end of each pincer too, dragging out two little points to form the scorpion's claws.

Viking Ship

This is a striking and difficult design with real wow-factor. This really relies on you keeping a very steady hand while pouring, so you might want to practise each individual pour before tackling the whole thing together.

1 Hold the cup with the handle facing away from you. Start by creating your base (see page 7) and fill your cup half full. Pour a small two-layered tulip (see page 18) into the centre of the cup.

2 Add a third layer to the tulip, but instead of lifting up, turn it into a rosetta (see page 12) moving down toward the edge of the cup.

Turn the cup around so the handle is now facing you. Pour a four-layered tulip into the centre of the cup so that it pushes up against the bottom of the tulip/rosetta on the other side. Finish the tulip with a line poured through the middle.

3

4

Pour a thin line from one side of the bottom layer of the tulip (the layer that is in the middle of the poured design) and finish it with a small heart (see page 9) near to the edge of the cup.

5

Repeat on the other side of the bottom layer of the tulip.

6

Turn the cup so the handle is now facing 3 o'clock. Pour a small two-layered tulip, starting halfway up the cup at the point where the original tulip and rosetta meet and moving at a right angle to the pattern you just poured, toward the handle. Finish this mini tulip with a little poured line through the middle.

8

Then twist the cup so the handle is now facing 11 o'clock and mirror this on the other side of the cup with two more mini tulips around the outside. Set the cup down in front of you with the handle facing to the right and you should have an intricate and perfectly symmetrical pattern which looks like the prow of a viking ship with its reflection in the water beneath.

7

Repeat this mini tulip pattern halfway between the first mini tulip and the rosetta at the bottom of the cup.

This is an elegant design which needs real pouring expertise – make sure you've perfected your vortex tulip before getting started on your final design.

Peacock in a Garden

1 Prepare two espresso cups of milk foam in white and red, following the instructions on page 60. Next, take a larger coffee cup and, with the handle facing away from you, create your base (see page 7) and fill your cup half full.

2 Turn the cup so the handle is now facing toward 4 o'clock. Pour a vortex tulip (see page 24) around the edge of the cup to about halfway around, twisting the cup as you go. Finish it by dragging a line down the inner side of the vortex tulip.

3 Turn the cup so the handle is now facing you. On the opposite side of the cup to the vortex tulip, pour two tiny rosettas (see page 12) at a right angle to each other to form a little semi-circle.

4 Pour three tiny little hearts (see page 9) into the centre of the semi-circle formed by the rosettas. This should leave you with a small rose pattern.

5 Turn the cup so the handle is now facing 4 o'clock. In the gap between the vortex tulip and the little rose, pour a rosetta all the way across the mug, curving around the flower as you pour. Finish the rosetta by drawing a line back up the side of it and curling it round at the top to create a little frond-like swirl.

6 With the pouring finished, set down your cup with the handle facing toward 3 o'clock. Use an etching tool to drag the rose petals into points (see page 61).

7 Drag a thin little stem down from the bottom of the rose and then draw on a couple of leaves, using white milk foam as needed.

8 Use the etching tool to drag a slender neck from the point of the largest layer of the vortex tulip. Curl it round at the end to form the head of the peacock. Pull down a beak from the head using more white milk foam.

9 Use a little red-coloured milk foam to add dots just above the head of the peacock as a crown.

10 Finally, use some white milk foam to draw a swirling line under the peacock and foliage.

TIP
You can carry on adding as much detail as you want to this scene, or leave it as is for a beautiful and intricate design.

Plum Tree ➤

This is another scenic design that combines skill with artistry. It's one of my favourite pieces of coffee art.

1 Prepare three espresso cups of milk foam in white, red and purple, following the instructions on page 60. Next, take a larger coffee cup and, with the handle facing away from you, create your base (see page 7) and fill your cup half full.

2 First, create the tree. Turn the cup so the handle is at 3 o'clock and pour an unfinished rosetta (see page 12) close to the top edge of the cup.

3 Turn the cup so the handle is now facing 11 o'clock and pour a second unfinished rosetta starting at the same point as the first rosetta, but moving in the opposite direction.

4 Pour a third unfinished vertical rosetta, starting from the point where the first two small rosettas meet, moving toward 5 o'clock and finishing about 1cm (½ inch) from the bottom edge of the cup.

5 Turn the cup so the handle is now facing 2 o'clock. Pour another unfinished horizontal rosetta at the base of the plum tree, starting close to the tree's base and then moving away to the right. Turn the cup so the handle is facing 9 o'clock, and repeat with another unfinished horizontal rosetta on the other side of the tree's base.

6

With the pouring finished, set down your cup with the handle facing toward 3 o'clock. Use an etching tool and some of the white milk foam to drag a line along the base of the rosetta on the right of the plum tree and then curve it up and round to make a swan's neck.

7

Use the etching tool and more white milk foam to draw in the swan's head. Repeat this with the rosetta to the left of the tree to create another swan.

8

Use the etching tool and some of the red-coloured milk foam to add red crests to the swans' heads.

9

Use some white milk foam to draw waves in the water beneath the swans.

10

Use the red-coloured milk foam to add some detail to the swans' bodies.

11

Use the handle end of a teaspoon to add blobs of purple-coloured foam to create the plums on the tree.

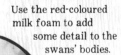

12

Add a dot of white milk foam to give each plum a reflective glint. You can also use the etching tool and more white milk foam to add a bird or two above the swans, by drawing small 'm' shapes.

Four Swans

This challenging free-pouring design is created with multiple rosettas, so practising the basic rosetta will help to develop your skills in this area. It requires a great deal of focus as the position of the cup changes five times as you pour the design.

TIP

Control is the key to this pattern as you need to ensure the swans' bodies do not merge together.

1

Hold the cup with the handle facing away from you. Start by creating your base (see page 7) and fill your cup half full. Pour a rosetta (see page 12), starting in the centre of the cup and moving toward 4 o'clock. Drag the finishing line along the top side of the rosetta.

2 Turn the cup so the handle is now facing you and pour a second rosetta opposite the first, leaving a 1cm (½ inch) gap between them.

3 Drag the finishing line along the top side of the rosetta and continue the stream of milk to create the swan's neck. Pour a small heart (see page 9) at the end of the neck for the swan's head.

4 Turn the cup so the handle is now facing 3 o'clock. Pour a third rosetta, starting about 1cm (½ inch) from the centre, at a right angle to the first two rosettas.

5 Drag the finishing line along the top side of the rosetta and continue the stream of milk to create the swan's neck and head as you did with the previous swan.

6 Turn the cup so the handle is facing 1 o'clock and add a swan's neck and head to the first rosetta.

7 Turn the cup so the handle is now facing 9 o'clock. Pour another rosetta at the fourth compass point, leaving a gap between the swans' bodies.

8 Drag the finishing line along the top side of the rosetta and continue the stream of milk to create the swan's neck and head as with the other swans.

Two Bunches of Grapes

This design is based on two slosetta shapes (see page 32), and requires all the elements of coffee art – pouring, etching and the use of colour.

1 Prepare four espresso cups of milk foam in white, purple, red and green, following the instructions on page 60. Next, take a larger coffee cup and, with the handle facing away from you, create your base (see page 7) and fill your cup half full.

2 Turn the cup so the handle is now facing 10 o'clock. For the first vine, slowly pour a slosetta (see page 32) starting at about 6 o'clock, close to the edge of the cup and curving round toward 3 o'clock.

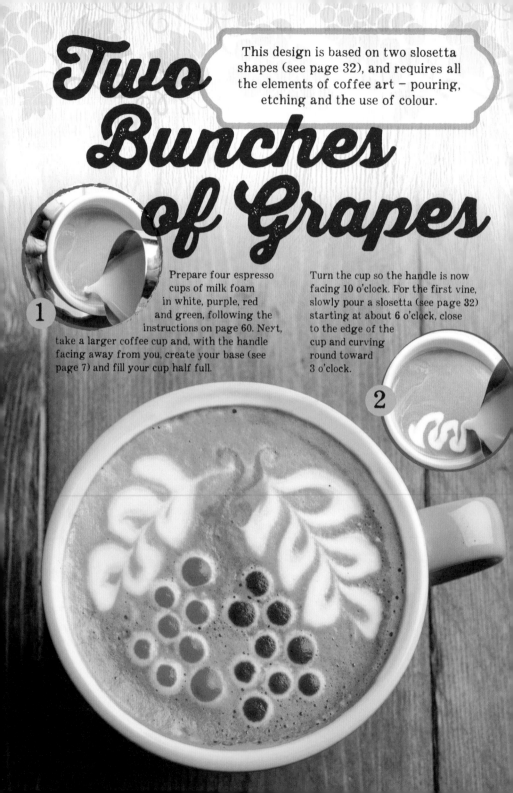

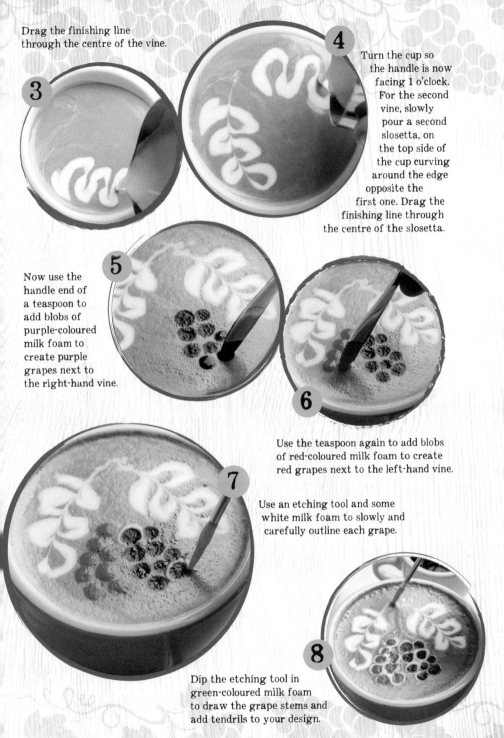

Drag the finishing line through the centre of the vine.

3

4

Turn the cup so the handle is now facing 1 o'clock. For the second vine, slowly pour a second slosetta, on the top side of the cup curving around the edge opposite the first one. Drag the finishing line through the centre of the slosetta.

5

Now use the handle end of a teaspoon to add blobs of purple-coloured milk foam to create purple grapes next to the right-hand vine.

6

Use the teaspoon again to add blobs of red-coloured milk foam to create red grapes next to the left-hand vine.

Use an etching tool and some white milk foam to slowly and carefully outline each grape.

7

8

Dip the etching tool in green-coloured milk foam to draw the grape stems and add tendrils to your design.

I like to think of this as a design with a surprise. With the first few pours, your audience will have no idea what the eventual design will be, and the regal Roman face appearing is always a crowd-pleaser. The etching is what really makes this design stand out, so practise on a piece of paper first before attempting it on coffee.

Roman Head

1 Pour a little milk foam into a small espresso cup to be used later. Next, take a larger coffee cup and create your base (see page 7) and fill your cup two-thirds full. Pour an unfinished seven-layered vortex tulip (see page 24) around the top edge of the cup.

2 Pour an unfinished rosetta (see page 12), starting in the centre of the cup and moving right toward 2 o'clock to make the laurel wreath for the Roman.

3 With the pouring finished, set down your cup with the handle facing toward 3 o'clock. Use an etching tool to pull a line through the centre of the vortex tulip, from the top of the cup to the bottom.

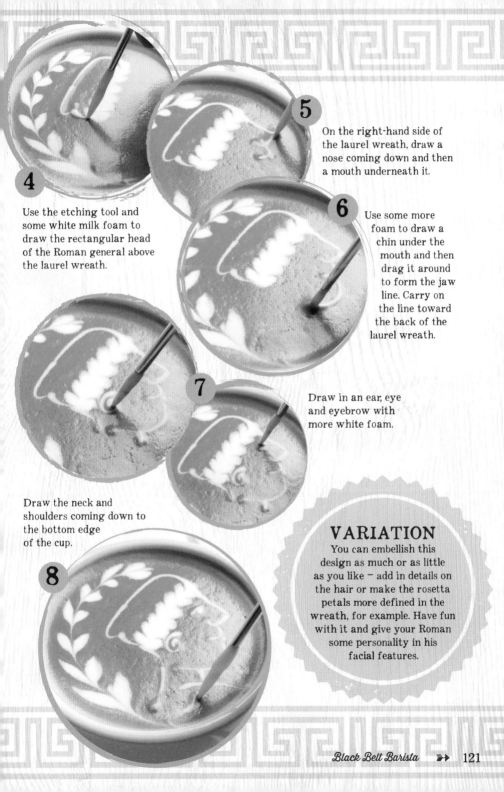

4

Use the etching tool and some white milk foam to draw the rectangular head of the Roman general above the laurel wreath.

5

On the right-hand side of the laurel wreath, draw a nose coming down and then a mouth underneath it.

6

Use some more foam to draw a chin under the mouth and then drag it around to form the jaw line. Carry on the line toward the back of the laurel wreath.

7

Draw in an ear, eye and eyebrow with more white foam.

8

Draw the neck and shoulders coming down to the bottom edge of the cup.

VARIATION

You can embellish this design as much or as little as you like – add in details on the hair or make the rosetta petals more defined in the wreath, for example. Have fun with it and give your Roman some personality in his facial features.

This design is based on rosettas along with some tulips to create the dragon's scales. You could add more colour details if you like – I've stuck to red for the fire in my version.

Dragon

Prepare two espresso cups of milk foam in white and red, following the instructions on page 60. Next, take a larger coffee cup and, with the handle facing toward 4 o'clock, create your base (see page 7) and fill your cup half full. Pour a rosetta (see page 12) along the bottom edge of the cup and finish by pouring a line along the inside edge of the rosetta.

2 Turn the cup so the handle is now facing you. Pour a second rosetta to mirror the first one on the other side of the cup.

3 Turn the cup so the handle is now facing 4 o'clock. Pour a final rosetta, starting in between the starting points of the other two rosettas. Stop pouring when you're around 2cm (¾ inch) from the edge of the cup and leave this rosetta unfinished.

4 Return to where you started the third rosetta and, on the top side of it, pour a small unfinished six-layered tulip (see page 18) very close to the final rosetta and moving toward the handle of the cup. These layers will form the scales on the dragon's neck. Now pour a line of milk from underneath the last tulip layer out to the right, then round, down and back underneath this line to create the dragon's head.

5 With the pouring finished, set down your cup with the handle facing away from you. Use an etching tool and some white milk foam to draw along the jawline to accentuate the chin. Pick up some of the darker coffee from the edge of the cup with the etching tool to draw a line for the dragon's mouth.

6 Add in some spikes and wisps of hair coming from the dragon's head using the etching tool and some white milk foam. Use the darker coffee and the etching tool to draw an eye and other details on the head.

7 Finally, etch some flames emanating from your dragon's mouth with some red-coloured milk foam – you can make this as dramatic as you want!

Intricate Pour with Two Swans

This is one of the most difficult designs in the book. You will need to have perfected your tulip pouring skills to create this symmetrical and elegant look. I've added in some etching on the swans but you can leave it as a poured design, which is just as impressive.

1 Pour a little milk foam into an espresso cup to be used later. Next, take a larger coffee cup and, with the handle facing away from you, create your base (see page 7) and fill your cup half full. Pour a four-layered tulip (see page 18) from the middle of the cup, moving out toward 3 o'clock.

2 Finish by pouring a line through the middle, which takes you back to the centre of the cup again.

3 Turn the cup so the handle is now facing you. Repeat the four-layered tulip, starting in the centre of the cup, and moving toward 3 o'clock again, so the two tulips are back to back.

4 Turn the cup so the handle is now facing 3 o'clock. For the first swan, pour a rosetta (see page 12), starting in the centre of the cup again and moving at a right angle to the first two tulips toward the edge of the cup at 3 o'clock. Finish the rosetta by pouring a line down its top side.

5

Turn the cup so the handle is now facing 9 o'clock and draw a rosetta (the second swan) on the other side, again finishing by pouring a line down the top side.

6

With your hand in the same position, pour an unfinished four-layered tulip along the top edge of the cup.

Turn the cup so the handle is now facing 3 o'clock again and do exactly the same opposite the tulip you have just poured.

7

8

With the pouring finished, set down your cup with the handle facing 3 o'clock. Use the etching tool to drag a line down the inside edge of the four unfinished tulip layers on each side of the cup.

9

Use the etching tool and some white milk foam to draw a neck up from the body of the swan on the left and curl it round to form a head. Repeat for the swan on the right-hand side. Finally, add three little dots above the head of each swan and draw a line down from each dot to the swan's head and join them together to form a crown.

Index